Two Homes to Live In

A Child's-Eye View of Divorce

Story by Barbara Shook Hazen

Illustrated by Peggy Luks

HUMAN SCIENCES PRESS

72 Fifth Avenue   3 Henrietta Street
NEW YORK, NY 10011 ● LONDON, WC2E 8LU

Library of Congress Catalog Number 77-21849
ISBN: 0-87705-313-8
Copyright © 1978 by Human Sciences Press, 72 Fifth Avenue
New York, N.Y. 10011

Printed in the United States of America
 9   98765432

3543

Library of Congress Cataloging in Publication Data

Hazen, Barbara Shook.
 Two homes to live in.

 SUMMARY: A little girl explains how she came to
terms with her parents' divorce.
 1. Divorce--Juvenile literature. 2. Children of
divorced parents--Juvenile literature. (1. Divorce)
I. Luks. Peggy. II. Title.
HQ814.H34   301.42'84   77-21849
ISBN 0-87705-313-8

For my son
Brack
who's been through
it all and is doing
nicely—
and for everyone
else going through
bad times, before
the better ones

Hi! My name is Niki.
My mommy and daddy are divorced.
That means they aren't married any more.

They are divorced from each other.
But not from me.
  My mommy is still my mommy.

My daddy is still my daddy.
And always will be.

When I was a baby,
Mommy and Daddy were married.

When I was little,
we lived in one place.
We were one family.

Then something happened.
Mommy and Daddy started acting
like they didn't like each other.

They acted like they didn't feel like friends.
Sometimes they got mad at each other.
Sometimes they didn't talk at all.
  One night they had a terrible fight.
I felt sad and scared inside.

The next day Daddy hugged me hard.
He said he was going to leave.
He said he was going to live
someplace else.

He said it was because he and Mommy
hadn't gotten along for a long time.
I asked Daddy if he was leaving
because of something bad I did.

Daddy said he wasn't leaving
because of **anything** I did.
He said it was all because
of grown-up problems.
He said, "Your mommy and I aren't happy
the way we wanted to be."
Then he held me very tight
and said he loved me very much
and always would love me
and always would be my daddy.

After Daddy left, I felt awful.
I sat on Mommy's lap.
She said she felt awful too.
   She said, "Sometimes grown-ups
just can't get along
no matter how hard they try."
   She said, "Sometimes grown-ups
fall out of love with each other.
But they never fall out of love
with their children."

"Why?" I wanted to know.
"Because it's different,"
said Mommy.
"Because I will always love you.
And Daddy will too."
"Even if I'm naughty?" I asked.
"Always and ever," said Mommy.
"No matter what you do.
Daddy and I will always love you."

At dinner I felt sad.
I couldn't stop looking at the daddy chair.

I missed daddy pancakes on Sunday.
And Mommy made me mad because she was busy.
Nothing seemed the same.

Soon after daddy picked me up.
He took me to a strange place.
He said it was his new home.
He said it was my home when I was with him.
 There was a bed and a bear there for me.
But it wasn't the same bed and bear.
And I missed Mommy.

On Sunday we had daddy pancakes.
I asked Daddy when he was coming home.
  He said, "This is my home now."
  Then he said he and Mommy
were going to get a divorce.
  "What's a divorce?" I asked.
  "Divorce means Mommy and I
won't be married any more," said Daddy.
"It means you will have two homes –
one with Mommy and one with me,
and pajamas both places."

"That isn't what I want!" I said.
"I want us to be one home and one family."
"I'm sorry," said Daddy. "But things
just aren't going to work out the way
you want, for grown-up reasons."
"Then I don't want any more daddy pancakes,"
I said. "And I want to go home and I want Mommy."

But when I was with Mommy,
I wanted Daddy. I missed him.
Everything was all wrong.
   One day I told Mommy,
"I think divorce is dumb!"
   "Divorce **is** sad," she said.
"But sometimes sad things
make people happier in the long run."
   She said someday I'd understand.
Someday seems so long.

After the divorce, I felt sad a lot.
  One night at Daddy's, I had a bad dream.
Daddy turned on all the lights
and hugged me tight and held me.
  "Bad dreams happen," he said,
"But the bad things that happen
in them aren't real."
  After a while, I went back to sleep.

Once when Mommy and I were making cocoa,
I started to cry and couldn't stop.
  Mommy said it was good to cry.
She said, "Tears wash away sad feelings
and let good feelings grow,
the way rain makes flowers grow."
  I felt better after.

Sometimes I had scary thoughts.
One time when Daddy was late, I thought
what if he doesn't come at all?
I thought, what if something bad
happened to him?

When I saw Daddy, I told him my thoughts.
He said he couldn't help being late,
just the way I couldn't help having scary
thoughts.

He said everybody has scary thoughts
sometimes. And it helps to tell them.

He said scary thoughts don't make scary
things happen because thoughts **can't**
make **anything** happen.

Then he gave me an extra long shoulder ride.

After the divorce, I started wishing
Mommy and Daddy would get married again.
I wanted us to be one family,
the way we were.
    When Daddy came to pick me up,
I hid so he'd have to be with Mommy.
I tried to make him stay.

I got mad when Mommy went out
with someone who wasn't my daddy.
I cried and tried to make her stay.

One day I told Daddy,
"I wish you and Mommy
would get married again."
    Daddy said, "Wish for something else,
because your mommy and I
aren't going to get married again."
    So I did. I wished for a kitten like Kim's.

When Mommy asked me what I wanted
for my birthday, I told her my wish.
   Mommy said, "I'm sorry,
but that wish can't come true.
Wish for something that can."
   So I wished for a bike like Benjy's.

    After a while I stopped
thinking about the divorce so much.
    After a while I stopped
feeling so sad.
    Daddy and I did special things.
at his place.
Once he let me make the pancakes.

Once we went rock climbing with my cousins.
    I didn't mind the divorce so much
after a while.

Mommy and I did special things, too.
We made a bookcase for my room.
I painted it all by myself.
I never did that with Daddy.

Once we went to a Chinese restaurant
with Uncle Harry and Aunt Katie.
We drank tea and ate with funny things
and everyone got the giggles.

I know a lot more about divorce now.
Having divorced parents isn't so bad.
Lots of kids do.
    Besides, nobody divorced me.

Having divorced parents means
having two homes and two families.
It means different ways of doing things
and different kinds of Christmas trees.

Having divorced parents means
pajamas both places,

and getting two sets of birthday presents.
Last week on my birthday,
I got a bike from Mommy
and a kitten from Daddy.

Sometimes I still think about the divorce.
Sometimes I'm still sad.
  But most of the time I'm happy
when I'm with Daddy
and when I'm with Mommy
and most of all with me.